SAVING GUS

Written by

Salma Rehman

Illustrated by

Omar Rehman

To order additional copies of this book, contact:
Xlibris Corporation
1-888-795-4274
www.Xlibris.com
Orders@Xlibris.com

For my wonderful and beloved brother
Imran
He is always in my prayers,
Salma

"Come on Eddie, we have to go home. Mom will be mad." Jena reminded her brother.

"No Jena, I want to play some more. It's summer break. Mom won't be mad". Eddie replied.

Mommy and Daddy Whale had never allowed them to be outside for so long, especially in this part of the ocean.

The only reason Mommy and Daddy Whale didn't want them to play here was Bob the Shark. He lived in this neighborhood .He was a mean shark, but his son Sharky was Eddie and Jena's best friend. He was a good kid. Their other friend Shayla the squid also came with them to play here. All four of them were friends since Kindergarten.

Eddie, Jena and Shayla always liked to sneak in here to play with their friend Sharky. It was no fun playing without him. There were lots of rocks in this area, so it was a perfect place to play hide and seek.

They were having a good time. It was Shayla's turn to be the seeker. Eddie was hiding behind a big rock when he heard a strange sound. He looked around him, but didn't see anything. He asked his friends if they heard something too. Sharky and Shayla also heard a groaning sound. "Guys, I think it's coming from behind that big rock." Sharky said. They all followed the sound, and were surprised to see what was behind that big rock.

"It's a huge sperm whale."Shayla shouted. She was scared of that giant creature.

"My parents have always told me to stay away from sperm whales. They are dangerous."

They all wanted to look at the sperm whale closely.

The huge, gray sperm whale was trapped in a big fishing net. He looked tired and in pain.

Some parts of the net were stuck in his skin. He also looked short of breath. He was trapped in the net so bad that he couldn't move.

"Who are you?" Eddie asked him. "My name is Gus. I got trapped in this net. I tried to get out, but I kept getting more and more trapped. Please help me." Sperm whale said in a low and deep voice.

Eddie and his friends felt so sad for Gus. He was in a lot of pain. "I am in pain and tired. The most important thing is that I am loosing oxygen. I haven't been to the surface in two hours. I need to breath really bad or I will not survive." All four friends tried their best to free him, but the net was very strong and tight. "I think we'll have to get our parents to help Gus." said Jena,

"Yes, you are right. This job is too big for us." Eddie agreed. They promised Gus to be back soon, and swam fast to their home. Sharky stayed with Gus to make sure he is ok.

Very soon, everybody was back to help Gus. Mommy and Daddy whale tried their best to get Gus out of the net, but they were unable to cut the strong net. Gus was getting weaker and weaker. He needed to breath really bad. All of them were feeling helpless.

They all knew who can really help Gus. It was Bob, The shark. It will be easy for the Bob to cut this net with his strong and sharp teeth. They were all scared to ask Bob for help. They all looked at Sharky, who had the same idea.

"Don't worry guys; I know my dad can help Gus". He is not as mean as you all think. My dad is a real nice guy." Sharky said. He left to get his dad.

When Sharky got home, Bob the shark was playing cards with his friends. Sharky looked panicky. Bob the shark asked, him. "What is wrong son? Are you ok? "I am fine dad, but I need your help."

"Son, can't you see I am busy right now." "Ba—but dad, please Gus the sperm whale will die if you don't help him." Sharky pleaded. "What are you talking about? Who is this Gus?"

Then Sharky told him the whole story. Bob the shark was still in no mood to help Gus, But Sharky kept begging "please dad for me, just for me" Sharky's eyes were filled with tears. "I want people to like you, not to be scared of you, please. You can do something nice for once and save Gus's life."

Bob the shark loved his son Sharky very much. He could not see him crying. He decided to help Gus.

Everyone was so happy to see bob and Sharky. Bob the shark saw Gus and started cutting the net with his sharp teeth. He had to bite really hard to cut the strong net. Gus's condition was getting worse. Bob kept biting the net as fast as he could. Everyone was watching it quietly. They couldn't believe their eyes. They had never seen Bob, the shark helping anyone before. Finally, he was able to get Gus out of the net.

Everybody cheered. They were all very happy for Gus and thankful to bob. Gus was extremely grateful to bob for saving his life. Mommy and Daddy whale helped Gus to the surface.

When Gus got to the surface, he took a deep breath, and he felt better.

Gus was still feeling very weak and hungry. Mommy whale asked him to go with them to their home so she can give him some food. She also invited Bob the shark and everyone else to come for dinner.

No one was scared of Bob any more. Now he was a friend to all. Sharky was relieved that nobody will call his dad mean anymore. "I am very proud of you dad" Sharky told his dad as he hugged him.

The end

www.ingramcontent.com/pod-product-compliance
Lightning Source LLC
Chambersburg PA
CBHW060828290526
45792CB00005BB/1846